KEVIN GARNETT

KEVIN GARNETT
"DA KID"

John A. Torres

LERNER SPORTS
A DIVISION OF LERNER PUBLISHING GROUP

This book is dedicated to my wife, Julie, and my children, Danny and Jackie, for their constant love, support, and ability to make me laugh.

Thanks to W.B. for the computer help.

This book is available in two editions:
Library binding by LernerSports
Soft cover by First Avenue Editions
Divisions of the Lerner Publishing Group
241 First Avenue North, Minneapolis, Minnesota 55401

Website address: www.lernerbooks.com

Library of Congress Cataloging-in-Publication Data

Torres, John Albert.
    Kevin Garnett : "Da Kid" / John A. Torres
      p. cm.
    Includes bibliographical references (p.) and index.
    Summary: Presents a biography of the Timberwolves forward who went
directly from high school basketball to playing in the National
Basketball Association.
    ISBN 0—8225—3673—0 (alk. paper). — ISBN 0—8225—9843—4 (pbk. :
alk. paper)
    1. Garnett, Kevin, 1976— —Juvenile literature. 2. Basketball
players—United States—Biography—Juvenile literature.
[1. Garnett, Kevin, 1976- . 2. Basketball players. 3. Afro
-Americans—Biography.] I. Title
GV884.G3T67 2000
796.323'092—dc21
    [B]   98—50472

Manufactured in the United States of America
1 2 3 4 5 6 — JR — 05 04 03 02 01 00

Contents

Kevin took a giant leap—from the preps to the pros.

Making the Jump

A cold February wind whipped at Kevin Garnett as he entered the arena. He was too excited to notice the biting chill. Kevin, the first player in 20 years to go directly from high school to the National Basketball Association, was about to play against a legend.

Kevin tried to stay calm in the visiting team's locker room. He listened to music on his headphones as he got dressed in his Minnesota Timberwolves uniform. He made sure to put a rubber band around his wrist. Then he went through his normal routine of stretching and warming up before heading out onto the basketball court. Sold-out United Center in Chicago was buzzing. Excitement filled the air.

People, some of them former classmates, were curious to see how a former Chicago high school basketball player would do against the best player in the world. Even the Reverend Jesse Jackson, a civil rights leader and political figure, attended the contest. People everywhere were curious to see how this experiment would work.

The NBA is made up mostly of former college basketball players. Once a player graduates from college or applies for early admission into the NBA, he is eligible to be drafted by a team. Each NBA team chooses two players but often only one makes the team. If the high school kid, Kevin Garnett, made it to the pros and was good, then experts predicted more and more high school players would skip college and go right to the NBA.

About 550,000 boys play high school basketball in the United States each year. About 15,000 athletes play for college teams—a third of them in the top college group called Division I. There are just 348 players in the National Basketball Association. Since getting into the NBA is such a long shot, there would be a lot of high school players who would be missing out on a college education while failing to make a living in professional basketball.

Kevin often felt he was being tested in his first year.

Before Kevin, only four other players had jumped from high school to the NBA: Moses Malone, Darryl Dawkins, Bill Willoughby, and Shawn Kemp. Kemp had attended a junior college but he had not played basketball there.

Kevin was nervous, but there was another reason he had trouble concentrating. Just two days before the game, his friend Ronnie Fields had been hurt in an accident. Fields had been in a car accident while he and Kevin were in high school together, too.

9

Playing against Michael Jordan and the Chicago Bulls was a dream come true for Kevin.

Kevin was worried about his old friend and excited about his new opportunity.

Kevin had been steady but unspectacular during his 1995–96 rookie season. He was averaging around 6 points a game while playing 21 minutes. NBA games are 48 minutes long. Some players play between 38 and 40 minutes a game.

Kevin walked out onto the court and into the glare of the lights. He looked up at the championship banners hanging from the rafters. Then the crowd exploded into cheers and Kevin spun around. Michael Jordan walked onto the court.

"When they say Jordan's name, people go so crazy that you can't hear," said Kevin. "Just the crowd yelling put goosebumps on me.

"I'm just happy to be on the floor with the man," Kevin said. "You see a guy like that and you say, 'That's where I want to be.' You come in and meet guys that you admired your whole life. It's just a dream."

Kevin caught his first pass in the game and sank a short-range **jump shot.** Shortly after that, he finished a perfect **alley-oop.** Any pregame jitters that Kevin had felt soon vanished.

Kevin ran the floor, made crisp passes, tore down **rebounds,** and swung his elbows to protect the ball.

Most important, he scored points. Even though his team lost, Kevin had his best game as a professional up to that time. He finished the game with 20 points and 8 rebounds. Even Jordan was impressed.

"He has all the right tools," said Jordan of Kevin. "He has to work on consistency, possibly doing that every night. [He needs] the experience of playing in this league, making adjustments every night against different opponents."

Kevin's long arms, his ability, and his instincts earned him great reviews from others in the NBA. Most fans and experts predicted that Kevin would become a great player. Defending him is very difficult since he plays the **small forward** position. Tall players are often not quick enough to play small forward. Shorter players usually play that position while players who are nearly 7 feet tall, as Kevin is, usually play at the center or **power forward** spots.

Kevin gained admirers throughout the NBA in his first year. But no fans liked him more than the Minnesota fans. In the six years before Kevin arrived, the Timberwolves had never won more than 29 games in an 82-game season. They had never made the playoffs, and they were the only team in NBA history to lose at least 60 games for four straight seasons.

Many players, especially rookies, would be afraid to join a team with such a terrible history. But not Kevin. "I figured this was a place that wanted me, needed me, to make an impact," he said. "Maybe I can change that [history]."

The Minnesota fans liked Kevin right away. They began to call the friendly youngster "Da Kid." With his huge talent and his outgoing personality, Kevin offered a glimmer of hope for Minnesota fans.

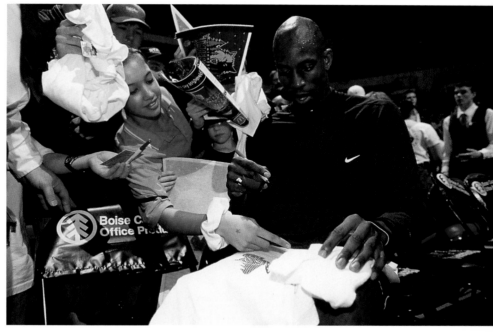

Fans of all ages want Kevin's autograph.

Kevin loved to play basketball whenever he could.

2

Growing Up

Kevin Maurice Garnett was born on May 19, 1976, in Greenville, South Carolina. Kevin's father, O'Lewis McCullough, and his mother, Shirley Garnett, were not married. When Kevin was seven, his mother married Ernest Irby. Kevin, his older sister Sonya, and his little sister Ashley lived with them. Five years later, the family moved to a house on Basswood Street in the small South Carolina town of Mauldin.

Kevin's father had been an excellent ballplayer as a young man. At 6-foot-4, he had been the captain of his high school basketball team. By the time Kevin was 12, he had grown to love the game also.

But Kevin's stepdad didn't like basketball. He wouldn't put up a hoop for Kevin in the family's driveway, so Kevin often went to play on the basketball courts at the nearby park. "When I didn't have a friend, when I was lonely, I always knew that I could grab that orange ball and go [play] hoops," Kevin said. "I could go and dunk on somebody. If things weren't going right, I could always make a basket and feel better."

Kevin's best friend, Jaime Peters, lived right across the street from him. Kevin and all his other friends called Jaime "Bug." Kevin and Bug were almost always together. Bug was happy to just hang out, but Kevin didn't like to waste time. He loved to practice.

Kevin worked on every part of his game—passing, jumping, rebounding, shot-blocking. Usually short players are more graceful than tall ones and have better balance. But even though Kevin was tall, he handled the ball well. Kevin told Bug that someday he wanted to play in the National Basketball Association. At the time, Kevin and Bug thought that was just a nice dream.

Bug and Kevin had many other friends in their neighborhood. A lot of kids who were about the same age grew up around Basswood Street in Mauldin.

Kevin's mother, Shirley Garnett, wanted Kevin to study and not just play basketball all the time.

Kevin and his friends listened to rap music and they loved to play video games. They all played basketball together. Kevin called his friends the "official block family." Desmond was the brain because he did well in school. Jerome and Andre lived a few blocks away. Baron "Bear" Franks was the oldest of the group, by about three years.

"We're like one big family," said Kevin, who always watched out for his little sister, Ashley, while their mother worked as a hair stylist. "We know each other's faults. We played ball together, we grew up with each other. We're like brothers. We're like peas and carrots, like peanut butter and jelly."

Another close friend in the group was Eldrick Leamon. Like Kevin, he was a great basketball player. Leamon wanted to earn a basketball scholarship to the University of Kentucky.

Kevin did not take his schoolwork seriously. He was too busy having fun with his friends. He would sneak out of his bedroom window to go play basketball or simply just "hang." His grades began to go down. Kevin's mother tried to keep a firm hand on Kevin but sometimes he fooled her.

When Kevin got to high school, he tried out for the basketball team. He didn't tell his mother that he was going to play basketball. She didn't find out he had made the team until the season started. Although Kevin's mother didn't encourage his playing, his coach did. "I knew he was gifted the first time I saw him on the court," said Mauldin High School coach James "Duke" Fisher. Kevin made Mauldin High's team. During his freshman year, Kevin scored an average of 12.5 points, had 14 rebounds, and blocked 7 shots a game. He also began a pregame ritual. Before every game he plays, Kevin puts a rubber band around his wrist or ankle.

Coach Fisher told Kevin that scoring was the easiest part of the game. He said that a player who is hot and still passes the ball to an open teammate truly has an all-round game. Kevin listened to his coach.

"I'd bust him at basketball practice, I mean really bust him," said Fisher. "And then he'd go to the park and play basketball there. He'd leave one practice and go practice again."

During the summer of 1992, between his first and second years in high school, Kevin began playing summer league basketball for Darren "Bull" Gazaway. Kevin's summer league team did well, and Kevin's game improved, too. "Kevin could have averaged 30 points a game, easy," said Gazaway, "but he didn't. He probably averaged about 18 points. He would pass, set up the other players. He was not stingy. He just loved to play the game."

Kevin became one of the best-known high school players in the country. Sometimes ESPN, a sports cable network, showed highlights of Kevin's games.

In the spring of his sophomore year, Kevin's phone rang. A 15-year-old New York City high school all-star named Stephon Marbury was calling. He had seen Kevin's phone number on a list of high school all-stars who had attended basketball camps. Stephon wanted to talk to Kevin since they seemed to have a lot in common.

The two high school stars hit it off immediately. They shared a lot of the same successes, problems, and pressures. Soon, they were talking regularly.

"Stephon served as a listener," recalled Kevin's mother. "He was someone who was there for Kevin. Kevin loves everyone and tries to please everyone.

But Stephon was the one who was telling Kevin to work hard academically and athletically."

The two became best friends without ever seeing each other. They talked so much on the telephone that Kevin's mother threatened to block long distance calls because the phone bill was so high. Kevin did not want to stop talking to Stephon so he got a job at a local Burger King to help pay for the calls. "Kevin's first week at Burger King, he had to give me half of his paycheck," said his mom with a laugh.

Marbury wanted his friend to join him in New York and play for his summer league team. Kevin's mother said that Kevin was already playing a lot of basketball. She did not want him going to New York all alone. Kevin stayed in Mauldin and played summer league ball again. He also went to Chicago to play in a summer basketball camp sponsored by Nike. His coach there, William Nelson, remembers thinking that Kevin was too skinny to be any good. Coach Nelson changed his mind after Kevin led his team to victories in 13 of its 14 games that week.

After the camp, Kevin headed back to Mauldin for his junior year in high school. It would be an important year for Kevin, on the court and off.

Kevin was almost always taller than his opponents.

3

Moving Away

By Kevin's junior season, basketball fans from all around Mauldin knew about him. The Mavericks' games sold out, so people came and stood in the hallways outside the gym, just to listen to the action.

Coaches from colleges all over also came to the games. Sometimes college coaches offer a talented player a scholarship. Most people thought that Kevin had the talent to be offered a scholarship. But to receive a college scholarship, a high school athlete must score above a certain level on the Scholastic Aptitude Test (SAT) or the American College Test (ACT). A coach can't offer a scholarship to an athlete who gets a low score on these tests.

History teacher Janie Willoughby was a good friend to Kevin at Mauldin High School.

Kevin still wasn't very interested in working on his school work or studying for the college-entrance exams. His history teacher, Janie Willoughby, tried to encourage him. She helped him sort through the mail he received from college coaches and she let him take quick naps in a corner of her room. Kevin worked hard in her class and did well, but he slacked off in his other courses.

Once Kevin had to give a report on a paper he had written for her class. He easily remembered all the facts and points he had made, but every so often he would look over at his teacher and ask, "Is that enough for a 'B' yet?"

"No, no, no," she would answer. "Just keep going."

Although his classroom work didn't improve, his

basketball playing did. Kevin had a tremendous junior season. He averaged 27 points, 17 rebounds, and 7 blocks a game. His team made it to the upper-state championship. Coaches contacted him, fans wanted his autograph, and the big shoe companies invited him to play at their summer camps.

The summer camps are showcases for the best high school players and are jam-packed with college scouts and coaches. There are many camps but Adidas and Nike sponsor the two best-known camps.

Kevin and Stephon had talked on the phone about the summer camps. They wanted to play together, but Stephon finally decided he would go to the Adidas camps. Kevin said he was going to play in the Nike league where he had played the year before.

In May, before school was out, a fight broke out at Kevin's high school. Several black students were hurt and a white student broke his ankle. Some people at the scene said Kevin had been in the fight. Others said that he had just been watching it. At nearly 7 feet tall, Kevin was very easy to spot. He and four other boys were arrested. Kevin says that he was not involved in the fight. He says he was passing by and stayed to watch. "I was only rubber-necking," Kevin said. "I was just walking by."

Duke Fisher taught biology and coached basketball.

Police called Kevin's mother at her hair salon and she rushed down to the police station. She found Kevin, in handcuffs and in tears, swearing that he was innocent. Kevin and the four other boys who had been arrested were sent to an intervention program and the charges against them were dropped.

"Just knowing Kevin like I do," said Murray Long, a white player who was on the Mauldin team with Kevin, "I don't think he would ever do anything to hurt anyone. When someone told me Kevin was arrested, I kind of laughed. I just didn't believe it."

Kevin felt like the students and teachers—even his coach—at his school began to treat him differently after the fight. Kevin and Coach Fisher had never been close but Kevin had often looked to him for guidance. Kevin began to feel like an outsider. "He never talked about it," said his friend Bear, "but I know he felt really betrayed."

Kevin's mother was upset, too. She did not like Kevin being involved with the police, and she didn't like his grades. "I knew we had to leave Mauldin," she said. "I knew we didn't have much time."

Marbury wanted Kevin to go to New York and play his senior year at Lincoln High School with him. Kevin's mom thought about that idea. The move would definitely cut out the long distance phone bills but it might not improve Kevin's poor study habits. Kevin was struggling in school and she did not want any more distractions in his life.

The summer of 1994, while Kevin and his family were thinking about what they should do, Kevin went back to Nike's all-star basketball camp. Not many of the coaches had ever seen a big player with the speed, power, and grace Kevin had. He handled the ball like a **point guard.** He rebounded like a power forward, and he made **three-pointers** like a small forward. In the **lane,** Kevin played like a center. He was a complete player at every position.

William Nelson, Kevin's coach at Nike camp, was also a coach at Farragut Academy, a public school in Chicago. Farragut was known throughout the country as a basketball powerhouse. Coach Nelson wanted Kevin to go to Farragut Academy and play basketball. He told Kevin's mother that Kevin would be better off in a good basketball program.

Many people began saying that Kevin would get a free college education and maybe even have a chance at professional basketball one day. Finally, Kevin's mom agreed. She and Ashley would move to Chicago with Kevin.

The move was not without its problems. Chicago's neighborhoods were very different from the sleepy town of Mauldin. "Living there was total hell," Kevin says. "There were gangs, guns, crime. It was no fun."

Kevin, his mother, and sister lived in a one-room apartment in the same building as Coach Nelson. Kevin's mother took two jobs to support the family.

Bug came to visit Kevin in Chicago. "I know I couldn't have done what Kevin did," he said. "I visited him there, and man, what a difference."

Jaime Peters, Kevin's childhood friend, visited him in Chicago.

In a small town like Mauldin, most of the kids knew each other. In Chicago, Kevin and Bug were just two more faces in a big city. Kevin and his friend were not used to worrying about gangs and guns. Stephon also visited Kevin in Chicago. When the two phone friends finally met, they hugged, said a few words, and then went to play basketball.

Their first minutes on the court together were magical. Kevin spun off a low block and headed for the basket. Without really looking, Stephon saw him.

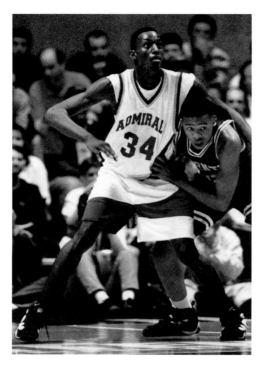

Kevin led Farragut's Admirals to a winning season.

He flung up a perfectly thrown, no-look, alley-oop pass that Kevin promptly slammed. The people in the gym howled with delight. Kevin was amazed at the instant chemistry he seemed to have with his friend. They were connected. They seemed to know what each other was thinking. After the game, the two friends ate lunch and talked about their dreams.

Kevin's grades improved as soon as he arrived in Chicago. Coach Nelson and his assistants made sure that Kevin concentrated on his studies. Kevin posted great grades, averaging a 3.8 (out of 4) in 13 core classes. But something else bothered him. He had not scored a high enough mark on the ACT to be eligible for a scholarship, even after he had taken a class to help students raise their test scores.

On the court, Kevin just got better and better. During his only season at Farragut, he averaged 26 points, 18 rebounds, 7 **assists,** and 6 blocked shots per game. He still played his unselfish style of basketball. "I'd be there yelling, 'Kevin, don't pass—shoot, shoot!'" said Coach Nelson.

Kevin teamed up with 6-foot-3 guard Ronnie Fields to lead the Admirals until Fields was injured in a car accident. Kevin led Farragut to a 28—2 record and the state tournament quarterfinals. He was named "Mr. Basketball" of Illinois and the National Player of the Year by *USA Today,* but still Kevin was discouraged. He wanted to go to college and play basketball. NCAA Division I colleges are not allowed to give a scholarship to or play any student who did not pass an entrance exam. Because of his low score, Kevin would have to sit out a full season before playing in college, if he could afford to go to college without a scholarship.

Marbury had scored well on the ACT and could choose from many colleges. He decided to attend basketball powerhouse Georgia Tech. Plenty of schools, including Maryland, Michigan, North Carolina, and South Carolina, had tried to recruit Kevin but they were waiting for him to score well enough on a college entrance test.

Kevin and the Admirals finally lost in the Illinois state playoffs.

After trying twice, Kevin had lost some confidence. He thought he might not be smart enough for college. "I was in a bind," he said. "Man, I wanted to go to college. I wanted to have options."

Kevin also had learned to not plan on the future. His friend, Eldrick Leamon, had died while they were still in high school when a car struck the motorcycle he had been riding. "So many people don't get to see that next day in life," Kevin said. "You can't take life for granted."

Kevin and his mother talked about Kevin's future. Kevin was afraid of getting lost or injured at a junior college. Plus, he began hearing from the experts that he was talented enough for the NBA. Still, very few players can play in the NBA without first playing college ball. Kevin felt a little more confident after many predraft predictions said that he was a sure first-round draft choice.

Kevin decided to declare himself eligible for the National Basketball Association draft. Then, just a few weeks before the June draft, Kevin got the results from his last ACT test. He had scored well. He was eligible for a scholarship to play college basketball. But Kevin had made up his mind. He was going to the NBA.

*Kevin had been a high school star, but was he really
ready to play against older, bigger professionals?*

A Popcorn Player

Kevin McHale played power forward for one of the greatest teams in the history of professional basketball. He had teamed with Larry Bird and Robert Parish to form the front line for the Boston Celtics in the 1980s. McHale was a ferocious rebounder and an unselfish team player. Throughout his playing days, McHale also learned how to judge other basketball players. He learned how to watch a player and know whether he could become an NBA star.

McHale retired from playing after the 1992—93 season and began working for the Minnesota Timberwolves. The Timberwolves had joined the NBA for the 1989—90 season. The team had struggled from the start. Bill Blair took over as head coach during the 1993–94 season, and the team finished 20–62.

Midway through the 1994–95 season, the team traded for forward Tom Gugliotta (GOOG-lee-ah-tah), a strong third-year player. Gugliotta gave Minnesota a boost, but the team still finished with a 21–61 record. After the season, the Timberwolves hired McHale as the vice president in charge of basketball operations. He was in charge of the coaches and the players.

McHale scouted all of the top college players who would be in the June 1995 NBA draft. There were a lot of good players, such as Jerry Stackhouse, Joe Smith, Rasheed Wallace, and Antonio McDyess. Then McHale watched Kevin play.

McHale knew that drafting Kevin, a high school player, would be taking a huge risk. What if the youngster couldn't stand up to the punishing 82-game NBA season? What if the older NBA players pushed him around? McHale saw the risks, but he also saw Kevin's potential. As a former forward, McHale thought he would be able to help Kevin develop his game. And, McHale thought, the Wolves could not sink much lower. The Timberwolves had the fifth pick in the 1995 draft. McHale gambled and chose Kevin.

Kevin shakes hands with NBA commissioner David Stern.

McHale hoped that Kevin would develop into what McHale calls a "popcorn player." He hoped that Kevin would become the kind of player who reaches his full potential when he arrives at the arena, hears the crowd, and smells the popcorn.

Kevin knew he would face a lot of pressure. Some players might resent Kevin's quick rise to the NBA. They might think he hadn't earned his NBA status. Kevin knew he would have to work hard, even harder than the other players did.

"I know people wanted me to fail," Kevin said, "but you've got to want to get better, and that's what really keeps me going. I want to get better every game I play. I want to show the world. I want to beat the odds."

According to an agreement between the NBA owners and players, a rookie's salary for his first three years in the league depended on his position in the draft. Because he was drafted fifth, Kevin signed a three-year, $5.6 million contract, making "Da Kid" very rich. After two years, the player and team could sign a new contract.

Some coaches worried that other high school stars might skip college in hopes of following in Kevin's footsteps. The people who run the NBA don't like the idea of a player going directly from high school to the pro league. But there wasn't much they could do to keep young players from applying for the NBA draft. "No knock on Mr. Garnett," said NBA deputy commissioner Russ Granik, "but obviously we'd prefer these kids play college ball, then join the league."

Kevin shook off the criticism and doubts. Confidently, he reported to training camp with his new teammates. Kevin wanted to remain a quiet person in the NBA, but from the first day of training camp, he felt that everyone was trying to test him.

"One of the things that I wanted people to under-stand was, I'm quiet, but don't ever try to show me up or bully me," Kevin said. "I wanted to set my foundation right there at camp, so people would know how to deal with me."

Kevin's mother had moved to Minnesota to live with her son, but she decided to go back to South Carolina. Ashley split her time between Mauldin and Minnesota, but Kevin's older sister, Sonya, moved near Kevin. She would check up on him, and some-times went to his house to cook for him. Kevin's old friend Bug moved in with him. The two friends spent most of their time playing music CDs and video games. Kevin was proud of the fact that kids and fans look to NBA players as role models. He didn't mind being someone's hero. "I don't drink or smoke or go out much at all," Kevin said. "I have an image to uphold. People are watching. Kids are watching."

On October 14, 1995, Kevin played in his first pro-fessional game. The Timberwolves were playing an exhibition game against the Milwaukee Bucks. Kevin put a rubber band around his ankle for luck. Then he went to work against Glenn "Big Dog" Robinson.

"In training camp, Kevin wasn't shooting," McHale said. "He wanted to work on other things. Then, when we played our first exhibition and he came out firing from everywhere, I knew we had our popcorn guy."

Kevin had a tough time guarding Robinson, and he realized that he still had a lot to learn about the game. McHale often practiced with Kevin, trying to get the younger player to use his body more to get open shots. McHale also worked with Kevin on his footwork. The closer a player is to the basket, the more important his footwork is. Kevin was a great outside shooter, but McHale wanted him to be able to move closer to the basket also.

Kevin poses with his sister Sonya and one of his nieces.

During the next few exhibition games, Kevin heard a lot of trash talk from opponents trying to rattle him. It didn't work. Trash talk was nothing new for Kevin. He didn't talk back or fight with them. Opponents banged elbows and hips into Kevin, hoping to provoke him into committing a foul or starting a fight and getting kicked out.

"When people start talking junk to me, I've heard it all in the park," Kevin said. "I think people thought I was weak or never heard that stuff. But my heart don't pump no Kool-Aid. This is all blood in here."

In a few exhibition games, Kevin showed that he was a good ball-handler and that he knew how to get the open shot or draw a foul. Still, he was young and inexperienced, so the Minnesota coach didn't give Kevin a major role in the Timberwolves offense when the regular season began. Coach Blair wanted to gradually work Kevin in so that his young star didn't feel too much pressure to score a lot.

Not having offensive plays called for him began to frustrate Kevin. That November, in another game against Milwaukee, Kevin got angry. He was having a tough time guarding Robinson again. Kevin wanted to show Robinson that he could score, too. But the coaches didn't call plays in which Kevin got the chance even though Kevin kept hollering for the ball. Finally, Coach Blair pulled him out of the game. "Coach Blair took me out because I was so mad," Kevin said. "I was screwed up in the head."

A few weeks into the season, Kevin started to feel more comfortable with his new teammates. Kevin's first big game came against the powerful San Antonio Spurs. Kevin outhustled every other player on the court. Kevin wound up with 19 points and 8 rebounds as the Timberwolves almost upset the Spurs.

In December, McHale decided the team needed a new coach. McHale hired Phil "Flip" Saunders, who had been coaching in the Continental Basketball Association, a minor league. McHale and Saunders had played together in college. Coach Saunders liked the way Kevin played. As the season went on, Coach Saunders put Kevin in the game more often and for longer stretches. The coaches began calling plays that gave Kevin a chance to score. By the middle of the season, Kevin was averaging 21 minutes, 6.4 points, and 4.2 rebounds a game. After the All-Star Game break, Kevin cracked the starting lineup and began to post impressive numbers.

One of Kevin's teammates, Christian Laettner, thought Kevin wasn't doing enough for their team.

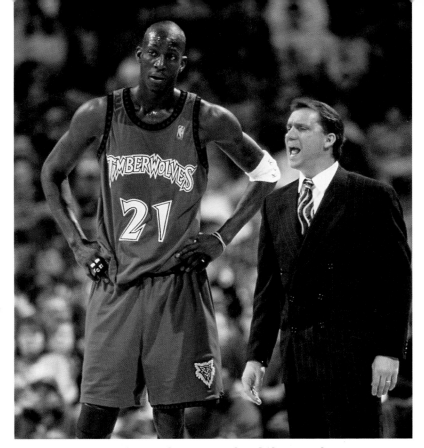

Kevin likes Timberwolves Coach Phil Saunders.

He criticized the young rookie, saying he was over-paid. Although Laettner was a talented forward, McHale didn't want him to create bad feelings on the team. He traded Laettner to Atlanta.

"To this day, I really didn't know he said something about me until the reporters brought it to me," Kevin said. "The only thing I wish I could have done was sit down with Christian and say, let's resolve this. Maybe the cold weather really got to him."

Kevin also kept in touch with Stephon at Georgia Tech. The two friends talked to each other often, encouraging and cheering for one another. Kevin made sure that McHale and the other Timberwolves officials knew how good Marbury was. He hoped that one day the two buddies would be on the same team.

Kevin averaged 14 points a game over the second half of the season. He was chosen for the All-Rookie second team. The Timberwolves finished the season 26–56, their second-best record. Although they did not make the playoffs, the Timberwolves would once again have the fifth pick in the NBA draft.

Stephon had decided to enter the 1996 draft even though it meant leaving college before he had a degree. Kevin told McHale that he thought the Timberwolves should pick Stephon.

Marbury had developed into one of the best point guards in the college game. His play impressed McHale, who told Kevin that he'd love to take Stephon in the draft. The only problem was that the Timberwolves would pick fifth. The Milwaukee Bucks, who had the fourth pick in the draft, also wanted to choose Marbury.

McHale contacted the Bucks general manager and

offered Minnesota's first pick and a future number-one draft pick for Marbury. The Bucks agreed. Kevin and Stephon were finally on the same team!

"I really want to be there," said Marbury. "I'm on cloud nine."

His tall buddy was just as excited. Next, Kevin thought, a spot in the playoffs!

Stephon Marbury grinned when Timberwolves general manager Kevin McHale chose him in the NBA draft.

5

Playoff
Payoff

With Gugliotta and Kevin as the sturdy forwards and Marbury running the offense as point guard, the Timberwolves started the 1996—97 season with high hopes. Coach Saunders found a way to use the talents of all three players while McHale kept working out with Kevin.

The work paid off. The Timberwolves started the season with three straight wins at home. In their fourth game, against the Los Angeles Clippers, Kevin and Marbury gave fans a taste of what to expect for the rest of the season. Kevin posted up against big forward Charles "Bo" Outlaw. Kevin saw Marbury with the ball, took one step toward him, and spun for the basket. Kevin caught Marbury's alley-oop pass in midstride and threw down a thunderous dunk. As the hometown crowd roared, the two friends gave each other a high-five at midcourt.

Although the Timberwolves were playing much better, they still struggled at times. On January 4, Kevin and Gugliotta each pulled down 13 rebounds, leading the Wolves to a 97—91 victory at Milwaukee. The victory was the second straight road win for Minnesota and boosted its record to 14—18. Some Timberwolves fans said the team might make the playoffs.

Kevin held his own against Michael Jordan and the other veterans in the 1997 All-Star Game.

By midseason, Kevin had become a versatile player. When Los Angeles center Shaquille O'Neal hurt his leg right before the All-Star Game, Kevin was asked to take his place. Kevin and Gugliotta were the first Timberwolves to play in an NBA All-Star Game. At 20, Kevin was the youngest all-star since Earvin "Magic" Johnson had made the team as a rookie.

When Kevin ran out on the court for the All-Star Game, he was very nervous. He kept hesitating until he caught a rebound and banked it in for two points. "I was glad 'Googs' was there," said Kevin. "I kept thinking, I'm all right as long as he's on the floor."

At the end of the game, Kevin caught the ball and kept it as he walked off the court. "It's the best souvenir of my career so far," Kevin said.

By April, the Timberwolves were playing well and had an excellent chance of making the playoffs. On April 4, the Wolves were playing the Washington Bullets. With the score tied and less than a minute to play, Washington's Chris Webber took the ball down low and seemed ready to score. Kevin came out of nowhere and jumped as high as he could to block the shot. Minnesota grabbed the rebound, scored a basket, and the Wolves had their third straight victory.

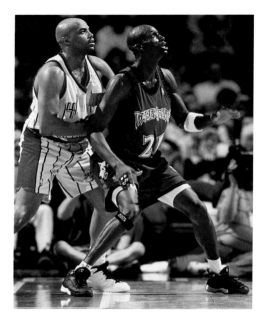

Charles Barkley and the Houston Rockets bounced the Timberwolves from the 1996–97 playoffs.

A few days later, on April 10, the Timberwolves defeated the Clippers, 108–96. When the final horn sounded, Marbury leapt into Kevin's arms. The Timberwolves had clinched a playoff spot! For the first time in the eight-year history of the team, the Minnesota Timberwolves would be in the NBA playoffs.

The Timberwolves had just squeaked in. As one of the lowest-ranked teams in the playoffs with a 40–42 record, Minnesota had to play Houston. The top-ranked Rockets swept the opening-round playoff series to end the Timberwolves' season.

Kevin finished the season averaging 17 points, 8 rebounds, and 2 blocks per game. Gugliotta had averaged 20.6 points and 8.7 rebounds and Marbury had 15.8 points a game. Fans thought the team's future looked bright with their three young players.

Under the NBA agreement, Kevin could play his third year with the Timberwolves and then go to whatever team would pay him the most money. Or, the Timberwolves could sign him to a longer contract before his third year in the league was over.

Timberwolves general manager Kevin McHale and Kevin celebrate their new, long-term agreement.

McHale and Timberwolves owner Glen Taylor did not want to risk losing Kevin. They agreed to pay him $126 million over six years.

Kevin's contract caused a lot of controversy. Other players who had played better and led their teams to more victories weren't given such rich contracts. Teams had to keep salaries under a certain limit. If they paid a lot of money to one player, they would have less to pay the other players. Some people did not think anybody should make that much money, no matter what he or she did.

Minnesota fans love Kevin's enthusiasm.

Despite the controversy about Kevin's huge contract, he remained popular with fans. Kevin often took time to sign autographs and greet his fans. He also is popular with the other NBA players. Kevin never plays dirty or argues with the referees. He just plays with good sportsmanship. "I want to be the best at what I do, not only as a player, but as a person," Kevin said. "Money shouldn't change you, or how you play the game. If something needs to be done, I'm going to try my best to do it."

At least in some ways, Kevin did not change. His favorite foods remained hamburgers, French fries, and pizza. His favorite book is *The Great Gatsby* and his favorite movie is either *The Show* or *Rebound*. In the offseason, Kevin had tried some acting. In the movie, *Rebound,* he appeared as Wilt Chamberlain, one of the greatest basketball players ever.

As the 1997–98 season began, the Timberwolves wanted to do more than just make the playoffs. They wanted to go beyond the first round.

In December, Kevin led his teammates to a victory over the SuperSonics—the first time Minnesota had ever beaten Seattle. In January, the Timberwolves beat Michael Jordan and the mighty Bulls, 99–95, for the first time in the Minnesota team's history.

Kevin notched his first career **triple double** in January with 18 points, 13 rebounds, and 10 assists in a 109–87 victory against the Denver Nuggets. In February, Kevin was chosen to start in the All-Star Game, the first time a Minnesota player had received that honor. He scored 12 points in the contest.

Throughout the season, Kevin made TV commercials for the NBA. In one ad, Kevin and several other NBA stars appear as ushers at an NBA game. They make adults in courtside seats move to the upper levels so that kids can sit in the courtside seats.

Gugliotta's season ended early when he injured his ankle, but Kevin improved as the season wore on. On March 29, he had 32 points, 14 rebounds, 6 assists, and 4 steals in a 104–96 victory over Sacramento. Kevin finished the regular season with averages of 18.5 points, 9.6 rebounds, and 4.2 assists a game. Not once in the 82 games did he score fewer than 10 points.

Even better, the Timberwolves had made the playoffs again, this time with a 45–37 record. Minnesota would play the powerful Seattle SuperSonics in the first round. The Sonics were heavily favored in the best three-out-of-five game series, especially since Gugliotta still could not play.

Kevin gave his best effort in the playoffs.

The SuperSonics couldn't stop Kevin in the first game of the series, in Seattle. Although he scored 18 points and grabbed 18 rebounds, the Wolves lost, 108−83. Game 2 was a different story. Coach Saunders used his quickest players and they outran the SuperSonics to win their first playoff game, 98−93.

The series then moved to Minneapolis, and the Timberwolves treated their hometown fans to another upset victory in Game 3. Kevin scored 19 points, grabbed 8 rebounds, had 6 assists, and blocked 3 shots. When Minnesota won, 98−90, the Timberwolves had a two-games-to-one lead.

If the Timberwolves could beat Seattle again in Minneapolis in Game 4, they wouldn't have to play again in Seattle. Kevin led his teammates by scoring 20 points, pulling down 10 rebounds, and giving out 5 assists. But the Timberwolves fell short, 92−88. The series went to Seattle for a deciding game.

Kevin wanted very much to win Game 5 and lead the Timberwolves to the next round. Maybe he wanted it too much. In Game 5, Kevin had one of the worst games of his career. He had scored in double figures for 86 straight games, but he scored just seven points in Game 5. He also committed 10 **turnovers.** The SuperSonics won, 97−84.

"What did I learn from this?" he said after the game. "I learned that sometimes you can get too hyped up. You can be too emotional. They were grabbing me and I just got frustrated and started forcing some things."

McHale and Taylor were disappointed by the loss in the playoffs and worried about the future. The team's contracts with Gugliotta and Marbury were almost up.

Seattle's Vin Baker consoles Kevin after the young Timberwolf played poorly and Minnesota lost.

Those players would ask for big contracts, like Kevin's. Would the Wolves be able to afford them?

Before the Timberwolves could begin their talks with Marbury and Gugliotta, all of the NBA owners and players had to agree to a new arrangement. The owners were worried that other players would get huge contracts like Kevin's, and teams would not make money. The players didn't want to limit how much a player could make. When the two sides couldn't agree, the owners locked out the players. No games would be played and players could not be signed or traded until an agreement was reached.

The 1998–99 season did not start when it was supposed to start. Finally, early in 1999, team owners and players agreed on a limit to player salaries. Teams and players were able to make deals. But the first big move was Michael Jordan's. The Chicago Bulls great retired from the NBA.

The next move affected the Timberwolves more directly. Gugliotta left to play for the Phoenix Suns. The Wolves picked up Joe Smith to fill Gugliotta's spot. Then Marbury decided he wanted to play near his family and friends in New York. So, the Timberwolves traded him to the New Jersey Nets. Terrell Brandon joined the Wolves to play point guard.

The teams played a shortened schedule in 1999, cramming 50 games into about three months. With so many new teammates, Kevin had to take on even more responsibility. He came through. He averaged almost 21 points a game as the Wolves slipped into the playoffs for the third straight year with a 25–25 record. But the turmoil had taken a toll on Kevin. At one point in the season, he was taken to the hospital after a game and had to stay there for two days.

The Timberwolves faced the formidable San Antonio Spurs in the first round. The Spurs and Utah Jazz had the best records in the NBA at 37–13. Once again, the Wolves were the underdogs.

The Spurs, led by Tim Duncan and David Robinson, won the first game of the series in San Antonio, 99–86. Despite being the underdogs, Kevin and the Wolves surprised the Spurs in Game 2, which was also played in San Antonio. Behind Kevin's 23 points and 12 rebounds, the Wolves upset San Antonio, 80–71.

Game 3 was played in Minneapolis. Kevin scored 23 points and had 12 rebounds again, but the Timberwolves played poorly for most of the game and lost 85–71. The Timberwolves had to win Game 4 to keep the series, and their season, alive. They could not do it. Kevin's 20 points and 16 rebounds were not enough and the Spurs won, 92–85.

Kevin was crushed. The Timberwolves were out of the playoffs after the first round again. Still, he knew he would have more chances at the title and he told his teammates and fans, "We'll be back."

Statistics

High School

	Points per game	Rebounds per game	Blocks per game
1991–92	12.5	14	7
1992–93	Not available	Not available	Not available
1993–94	27	17	7
1994–95	25.2	17.9	6.5
Totals	Points	Rebounds	Blocks
	2,533	1,807	739

National Basketball Association

Minnesota Timberwolves								
Year	Games	FGM	FGA	FTM	FTA	Rebounds	Blocks	Points
1995–96	80	361	735	105	149	501	131	835
1996–97	77	549	1,100	205	272	618	163	1,309
1997–98	82	635	1,293	245	332	786	150	1,518
1999	47	414	900	145	206	489	83	977
Totals	286	1,959	4,028	700	959	2,394	527	4,639

Glossary

alley-oop: A play in which one player passes the ball above the rim and another player catches the pass and slams the ball through the hoop.

assist(s): A pass to a teammate who then scores.

jump shot: A shot in which the shooting player jumps and releases the ball while in mid-air.

lane: The 12-foot wide area under the basket that extends from the end line to the free throw line.

point guard: A player whose primary job is to dribble the ball and run offensive plays.

power forward: A player whose primary job is to shoot and rebound.

rebound(s): Catching the ball after a missed shot.

small forward: A player whose primary job is to shoot, rebound, and dribble the ball.

three-pointers: Baskets that are shot from beyond the three-point line.

triple double: Scoring 10 or more points, passing for 10 or more assists, and grabbing 10 or more rebounds in a single game.

turnover(s): Losing the ball to an opponent.

Sources

Information for this book was obtained from the following sources: Steve Aschburner (*Inside Sports*, July 1996); Steve Aschburner (*NBA Inside Stuff*, May 1997 and July 1997); Steve Aschburner (*The Sporting News*, 9 May 1998); *Current Biography*, September 1998; Michael Farber (*Sports Illustrated*, 20 January 1997); Greg Guss (*Sport*, November 1996); Curry Kirkpatrick (*Newsweek*, 4 December 1995); Jack McCallum (*Sports Illustrated*, 26 June 1995); Leigh Montville (*Sport Illustrated*, 3 May 1999); Ellen Tomson (*St. Paul Pioneer Press*, 30 November 1998.

Index

Write to Kevin

You can send mail to Kevin at the address on the right. If you write a letter, don't get your hopes up too high. Kevin and other athletes get lots of letters every day, and they aren't always able to answer them all.

Kevin Garnett
c/o Minnesota Timberwolves
Target Center
600 First Avenue North
Minneapolis, MN 55401

Acknowledgments

Photographs reproduced with permission of: © ALLSPORT USA/Doug Pensinger, p. 1; © Layne Murdoch/NBA Photos, p. 2; © ALLSPORT USA, p. 6; © SportsChrome East/West/Rich Kane, p. 9; © ALLSPORT USA/Brian Bahr, p. 10; © David Sherman/NBA Photos, pp. 13, 51, 52; © Gwinn Davis/The Tribune-Times, pp. 14, 17, 20, 22, 40; © Seth Poppel Yearbook Archives, pp. 24, 26, 29; © Illinois High School Association, pp. 30, 32; © ALLSPORT USA/Todd Rosenberg, p. 34; © Scott Cunningham/NBA Photos, pp. 37, 46; © Gary Dineen/NBA Photos, p. 43; © Dale Tait/NBA Photos, p. 45; © Andy Hayt/NBA Photos, p. 48; © Glenn James/NBA Photos, p. 50; Reuters/Eric Miller/Archive Photos, p. 55; Reuters/Anthony Bolante/Archive Photos, p. 57.

Front cover photograph by © ALLSPORT USA/Nathaniel S. Butler.
Back cover photograph by AP/Wide World Sports.
Artwork by Michael Tacheny.

About the Author

John A. Torres is the author of sports books for young readers, including Lerner's *Greg Maddux*. John lives with his family in New York.